ILLUMINATED
SCRIPTURE JOURNAL

ENGLISH STANDARD VERSION

ACTS

CROSSWAY

WHEATON, ILLINOIS — ESV.ORG

RRDS	27	26	25	24	23	22	21	20	19
11	10	9	8	7	6	5	4	3	

PREFACE

The Bible

The words of the Bible are the very words of God our Creator speaking to us. They are completely truthful;[1] they are pure;[2] they are powerful;[3] and they are wise and righteous.[4] We should read these words with reverence and awe,[5] and with joy and delight.[6] Through these words God gives us eternal life,[7] and daily nourishes our spiritual lives.[8]

The ESV Translation

The English Standard Version® (ESV®) stands in the classic stream of English Bible translations that goes back nearly five centuries. In this stream, accurate faithfulness to the original text is combined with simplicity, beauty, and dignity of expression. Our goal has been to carry forward this legacy for this generation and generations to come.

The ESV is an "essentially literal" translation that seeks as far as possible to reproduce the meaning and structure of the original text and the personal style of each Bible writer. We have sought to be "as literal as possible" while maintaining clear expression and literary excellence. Therefore the ESV is well suited for both personal reading and church ministry, for devotional reflection and serious study, and for Scripture memorization.

---

[1] Ps. 119:160; Prov. 30:5; Titus 1:2; Heb. 6:18 [2] Ps. 12:6 [3] Jer. 23:29; Heb. 4:12; 1 Pet. 1:23
[4] Ps. 19:7–11 [5] Deut. 28:58; Ps. 119:74; Isa. 66:2 [6] Ps. 19:7–11; 119:14, 97, 103; Jer. 15:16
[7] John 6:68; 1 Pet. 1:23 [8] Deut. 32:46; Matt. 4:4

The ESV publishing team has included more than a hundred people. The fourteen-member Translation Oversight Committee benefited from the work of fifty biblical experts serving as Translation Review Scholars and from the comments of the more than fifty members of the Advisory Council. This international team from many denominations shares a common commitment to the truth of God's Word and to historic Christian orthodoxy.

To God's Honor and Praise

We know that no Bible translation is perfect; but we also know that God uses imperfect and inadequate things to his honor and praise. So to God the Father, Son, and Holy Spirit— and to his people—we offer what we have done, with our prayers that it may prove useful, with gratitude for much help given, and with ongoing wonder that our God should ever have entrusted to us so momentous a task.

To God alone be the glory!
The Translation Oversight Committee

ACTS

The Promise of the Holy Spirit

1 In the first book, O Theophilus, I have dealt with all that Jesus began to do and teach, ² until the day when he was taken up, after he had given commands through the Holy Spirit to the apostles whom he had chosen. ³ He presented himself alive to them after his suffering by many proofs, appearing to them during forty days and speaking about the kingdom of God.

⁴ And while staying with them he ordered them not to depart from Jerusalem, but to wait for the promise of the Father, which, he said, "you heard from me; ⁵ for John baptized with water, but you will be baptized with the Holy Spirit not many days from now."

The Ascension

⁶ So when they had come together, they asked him, "Lord, will you at this time restore the kingdom to Israel?" ⁷ He said to them, "It is not for you to know times or seasons that the Father has fixed by his own authority. ⁸ But you will receive power when the Holy Spirit has come upon you, and you will be my witnesses in Jerusalem and in all Judea and Samaria, and to the end of the earth." ⁹ And when he had said these things, as they were looking on, he was lifted up, and a cloud took him

1) Why Acts?
We see what the church is to be
about.
   Worship:

   Nurture:

   Mission:

We see a "real church." not perfect.
Evidence of abundance grace and favor of God
   for the church
   2) Background info...   — To the —
      ① Structure · Historical narrative END
                     · discriptive
                     condensed)   — OF THE —
                     Transitional
Movements)   EARTH

                                     ACTS 1:8
         ② Setting
Tools for the Task:
                    1) An energizing reality
                    2) A sufficient power supply
                    3) A simple mission
                    4) An urgent Motive

out of their sight. [10] And while they were gazing into heaven as he went, behold, two men stood by them in white robes, [11] and said, "Men of Galilee, why do you stand looking into heaven? This Jesus, who was taken up from you into heaven, will come in the same way as you saw him go into heaven."

Matthias Chosen to Replace Judas

[12] Then they returned to Jerusalem from the mount called Olivet, which is near Jerusalem, a Sabbath day's journey away. [13] And when they had entered, they went up to the upper room, where they were staying, Peter and John and James and Andrew, Philip and Thomas, Bartholomew and Matthew, James the son of Alphaeus and Simon the Zealot and Judas the son of James. [14] All these with one accord were devoting themselves to prayer, together with the women and Mary the mother of Jesus, and his brothers.

[15] In those days Peter stood up among the brothers (the company of persons was in all about 120) and said, [16] "Brothers, the Scripture had to be fulfilled, which the Holy Spirit spoke beforehand by the mouth of David concerning Judas, who became a guide to those who arrested Jesus. [17] For he was numbered among us and was allotted his share in this ministry." [18] (Now this man acquired a field with the reward of his wickedness, and falling headlong he burst open in the middle and all his bowels gushed out. [19] And it became known to all the inhabitants of Jerusalem, so that the field was called in their own language Akeldama, that is, Field of Blood.) [20] "For it is written in the Book of Psalms,

> "'May his camp become desolate,
>   and let there be no one to dwell in it';

Actually Waiting on God   Acts 1:12-26

1.) Obedience

2.) Prayer
3) Scripture authority

4) Confident trust (in God's sovereignty)

and

> " 'Let another take his office.'

²¹ So one of the men who have accompanied us during all the time that the Lord Jesus went in and out among us, ²² beginning from the baptism of John until the day when he was taken up from us—one of these men must become with us a witness to his resurrection." ²³ And they put forward two, Joseph called Barsabbas, who was also called Justus, and Matthias. ²⁴ And they prayed and said, "You, Lord, who know the hearts of all, show which one of these two you have chosen ²⁵ to take the place in this ministry and apostleship from which Judas turned aside to go to his own place." ²⁶ And they cast lots for them, and the lot fell on Matthias, and he was numbered with the eleven apostles.

The Coming of the Holy Spirit

2 When the day of Pentecost arrived, they were all together in one place. ² And suddenly there came from heaven a sound like a mighty rushing wind, and it filled the entire house where they were sitting. ³ And divided tongues as of fire appeared to them and rested on each one of them. ⁴ And they were all filled with the Holy Spirit and began to speak in other tongues as the Spirit gave them utterance.

⁵ Now there were dwelling in Jerusalem Jews, devout men from every nation under heaven. ⁶ And at this sound the multitude came together, and they were bewildered, because each one was hearing them speak in his own language. ⁷ And they were amazed and astonished, saying, "Are not all these who are

speaking Galileans? [8] And how is it that we hear, each of us in his own native language? [9] Parthians and Medes and Elamites and residents of Mesopotamia, Judea and Cappadocia, Pontus and Asia, [10] Phrygia and Pamphylia, Egypt and the parts of Libya belonging to Cyrene, and visitors from Rome, [11] both Jews and proselytes, Cretans and Arabians—we hear them telling in our own tongues the mighty works of God." [12] And all were amazed and perplexed, saying to one another, "What does this mean?" [13] But others mocking said, "They are filled with new wine."

Peter's Sermon at Pentecost

[14] But Peter, standing with the eleven, lifted up his voice and addressed them: "Men of Judea and all who dwell in Jerusalem, let this be known to you, and give ear to my words. [15] For these people are not drunk, as you suppose, since it is only the third hour of the day. [16] But this is what was uttered through the prophet Joel:

[17]   "'And in the last days it shall be, God declares,
            that I will pour out my Spirit on all flesh,
            and your sons and your daughters shall prophesy,
                and your young men shall see visions,
                and your old men shall dream dreams;
[18]   even on my male servants and female servants
                in those days I will pour out my Spirit, and they
                    shall prophesy.
[19]   And I will show wonders in the heavens above
                and signs on the earth below,
                blood, and fire, and vapor of smoke;

20   the sun shall be turned to darkness
          and the moon to blood,
              before the day of the Lord comes, the great and
                  magnificent day.
21   And it shall come to pass that everyone who calls
              upon the name of the Lord shall be
              saved.'

²² "Men of Israel, hear these words: Jesus of Nazareth, a man attested to you by God with mighty works and wonders and signs that God did through him in your midst, as you yourselves know— ²³ this Jesus, delivered up according to the definite plan and foreknowledge of God, you crucified and killed by the hands of lawless men. ²⁴ God raised him up, loosing the pangs of death, because it was not possible for him to be held by it. ²⁵ For David says concerning him,

    " 'I saw the Lord always before me,
          for he is at my right hand that I may not be
              shaken;
26   therefore my heart was glad, and my tongue rejoiced;
          my flesh also will dwell in hope.
27   For you will not abandon my soul to Hades,
          or let your Holy One see corruption.
28   You have made known to me the paths of life;
          you will make me full of gladness with your
              presence.'

²⁹ "Brothers, I may say to you with confidence about the patriarch David that he both died and was buried, and his tomb

is with us to this day. [30] Being therefore a prophet, and knowing that God had sworn with an oath to him that he would set one of his descendants on his throne, [31] he foresaw and spoke about the resurrection of the Christ, that he was not abandoned to Hades, nor did his flesh see corruption. [32] This Jesus God raised up, and of that we all are witnesses. [33] Being therefore exalted at the right hand of God, and having received from the Father the promise of the Holy Spirit, he has poured out this that you yourselves are seeing and hearing. [34] For David did not ascend into the heavens, but he himself says,

> "'The Lord said to my Lord,
> "Sit at my right hand,
> [35]   until I make your enemies your footstool."'

[36] Let all the house of Israel therefore know for certain that God has made him both Lord and Christ, this Jesus whom you crucified."

[37] Now when they heard this they were cut to the heart, and said to Peter and the rest of the apostles, "Brothers, what shall we do?" [38] And Peter said to them, "Repent and be baptized every one of you in the name of Jesus Christ for the forgiveness of your sins, and you will receive the gift of the Holy Spirit. [39] For the promise is for you and for your children and for all who are far off, everyone whom the Lord our God calls to himself." [40] And with many other words he bore witness and continued to exhort them, saying, "Save yourselves from this crooked generation." [41] So those who received his word were baptized, and there were added that day about three thousand souls.

The Fellowship of the Believers

⁴² And they devoted themselves to the apostles' teaching and the fellowship, to the breaking of bread and the prayers. ⁴³ And awe came upon every soul, and many wonders and signs were being done through the apostles. ⁴⁴ And all who believed were together and had all things in common. ⁴⁵ And they were selling their possessions and belongings and distributing the proceeds to all, as any had need. ⁴⁶ And day by day, attending the temple together and breaking bread in their homes, they received their food with glad and generous hearts, ⁴⁷ praising God and having favor with all the people. And the Lord added to their number day by day those who were being saved.

The Lame Beggar Healed

3 Now Peter and John were going up to the temple at the hour of prayer, the ninth hour. ² And a man lame from birth was being carried, whom they laid daily at the gate of the temple that is called the Beautiful Gate to ask alms of those entering the temple. ³ Seeing Peter and John about to go into the temple, he asked to receive alms. ⁴ And Peter directed his gaze at him, as did John, and said, "Look at us." ⁵ And he fixed his attention on them, expecting to receive something from them. ⁶ But Peter said, "I have no silver and gold, but what I do have I give to you. In the name of Jesus Christ of Nazareth, rise up and walk!" ⁷ And he took him by the right hand and raised him up, and immediately his feet and ankles were made strong. ⁸ And leaping up, he stood and began to walk, and entered the temple with them, walking and leaping and praising God. ⁹ And all the people saw him walking and praising God, ¹⁰ and recognized him as the one who sat at the Beautiful Gate of the

They **DEVOTED** THEMSELVES TO THE **APOSTLES' TEACHING** AND THE **FELLOWSHIP** TO THE **BREAKING** of **BREAD** AND THE **PRAYERS**

ACTS 2:42

temple, asking for alms. And they were filled with wonder and amazement at what had happened to him.

Peter Speaks in Solomon's Portico

¹¹ While he clung to Peter and John, all the people, utterly astounded, ran together to them in the portico called Solomon's. ¹² And when Peter saw it he addressed the people: "Men of Israel, why do you wonder at this, or why do you stare at us, as though by our own power or piety we have made him walk? ¹³ The God of Abraham, the God of Isaac, and the God of Jacob, the God of our fathers, glorified his servant Jesus, whom you delivered over and denied in the presence of Pilate, when he had decided to release him. ¹⁴ But you denied the Holy and Righteous One, and asked for a murderer to be granted to you, ¹⁵ and you killed the Author of life, whom God raised from the dead. To this we are witnesses. ¹⁶ And his name — by faith in his name — has made this man strong whom you see and know, and the faith that is through Jesus has given the man this perfect health in the presence of you all.

¹⁷ "And now, brothers, I know that you acted in ignorance, as did also your rulers. ¹⁸ But what God foretold by the mouth of all the prophets, that his Christ would suffer, he thus fulfilled. ¹⁹ Repent therefore, and turn back, that your sins may be blotted out, ²⁰ that times of refreshing may come from the presence of the Lord, and that he may send the Christ appointed for you, Jesus, ²¹ whom heaven must receive until the time for restoring all the things about which God spoke by the mouth of his holy prophets long ago. ²² Moses said, 'The Lord God will raise up for you a prophet like me from your brothers. You shall listen to him in whatever he tells you. ²³ And it shall be that every soul

REPENT THEREFORE AND TURN BACK

ACTS 3:19

who does not listen to that prophet shall be destroyed from the people.' ²⁴ And all the prophets who have spoken, from Samuel and those who came after him, also proclaimed these days. ²⁵ You are the sons of the prophets and of the covenant that God made with your fathers, saying to Abraham, 'And in your offspring shall all the families of the earth be blessed.' ²⁶ God, having raised up his servant, sent him to you first, to bless you by turning every one of you from your wickedness."

Peter and John Before the Council

4 And as they were speaking to the people, the priests and the captain of the temple and the Sadducees came upon them, ² greatly annoyed because they were teaching the people and proclaiming in Jesus the resurrection from the dead. ³ And they arrested them and put them in custody until the next day, for it was already evening. ⁴ But many of those who had heard the word believed, and the number of the men came to about five thousand.

⁵ On the next day their rulers and elders and scribes gathered together in Jerusalem, ⁶ with Annas the high priest and Caiaphas and John and Alexander, and all who were of the high-priestly family. ⁷ And when they had set them in the midst, they inquired, "By what power or by what name did you do this?" ⁸ Then Peter, filled with the Holy Spirit, said to them, "Rulers of the people and elders, ⁹ if we are being examined today concerning a good deed done to a crippled man, by what means this man has been healed, ¹⁰ let it be known to all of you and to all the people of Israel that by the name of Jesus Christ of Nazareth, whom you crucified, whom God raised from the dead—by him this man is standing before you well. ¹¹ This

Jesus is the stone that was rejected by you, the builders, which has become the cornerstone. ¹² And there is salvation in no one else, for there is no other name under heaven given among men by which we must be saved."

¹³ Now when they saw the boldness of Peter and John, and perceived that they were uneducated, common men, they were astonished. And they recognized that they had been with Jesus. ¹⁴ But seeing the man who was healed standing beside them, they had nothing to say in opposition. ¹⁵ But when they had commanded them to leave the council, they conferred with one another, ¹⁶ saying, "What shall we do with these men? For that a notable sign has been performed through them is evident to all the inhabitants of Jerusalem, and we cannot deny it. ¹⁷ But in order that it may spread no further among the people, let us warn them to speak no more to anyone in this name." ¹⁸ So they called them and charged them not to speak or teach at all in the name of Jesus. ¹⁹ But Peter and John answered them, "Whether it is right in the sight of God to listen to you rather than to God, you must judge, ²⁰ for we cannot but speak of what we have seen and heard." ²¹ And when they had further threatened them, they let them go, finding no way to punish them, because of the people, for all were praising God for what had happened. ²² For the man on whom this sign of healing was performed was more than forty years old.

The Believers Pray for Boldness

²³ When they were released, they went to their friends and reported what the chief priests and the elders had said to them. ²⁴ And when they heard it, they lifted their voices together to God and said, "Sovereign Lord, who made the heaven and the

earth and the sea and everything in them, ²⁵ who through the mouth of our father David, your servant, said by the Holy Spirit,

> " 'Why did the Gentiles rage,
>   and the peoples plot in vain?
> ²⁶   The kings of the earth set themselves,
>   and the rulers were gathered together,
>   against the Lord and against his Anointed'—

²⁷ for truly in this city there were gathered together against your holy servant Jesus, whom you anointed, both Herod and Pontius Pilate, along with the Gentiles and the peoples of Israel, ²⁸ to do whatever your hand and your plan had predestined to take place. ²⁹ And now, Lord, look upon their threats and grant to your servants to continue to speak your word with all boldness, ³⁰ while you stretch out your hand to heal, and signs and wonders are performed through the name of your holy servant Jesus." ³¹ And when they had prayed, the place in which they were gathered together was shaken, and they were all filled with the Holy Spirit and continued to speak the word of God with boldness.

They Had Everything in Common

³² Now the full number of those who believed were of one heart and soul, and no one said that any of the things that belonged to him was his own, but they had everything in common. ³³ And with great power the apostles were giving their testimony to the resurrection of the Lord Jesus, and great grace was upon them all. ³⁴ There was not a needy person among them, for as many as were owners of lands or houses sold them

and brought the proceeds of what was sold ³⁵ and laid it at the apostles' feet, and it was distributed to each as any had need. ³⁶ Thus Joseph, who was also called by the apostles Barnabas (which means son of encouragement), a Levite, a native of Cyprus, ³⁷ sold a field that belonged to him and brought the money and laid it at the apostles' feet.

Ananias and Sapphira

5 But a man named Ananias, with his wife Sapphira, sold a piece of property, ² and with his wife's knowledge he kept back for himself some of the proceeds and brought only a part of it and laid it at the apostles' feet. ³ But Peter said, "Ananias, why has Satan filled your heart to lie to the Holy Spirit and to keep back for yourself part of the proceeds of the land? ⁴ While it remained unsold, did it not remain your own? And after it was sold, was it not at your disposal? Why is it that you have contrived this deed in your heart? You have not lied to man but to God." ⁵ When Ananias heard these words, he fell down and breathed his last. And great fear came upon all who heard of it. ⁶ The young men rose and wrapped him up and carried him out and buried him.

⁷ After an interval of about three hours his wife came in, not knowing what had happened. ⁸ And Peter said to her, "Tell me whether you sold the land for so much." And she said, "Yes, for so much." ⁹ But Peter said to her, "How is it that you have agreed together to test the Spirit of the Lord? Behold, the feet of those who have buried your husband are at the door, and they will carry you out." ¹⁰ Immediately she fell down at his feet and breathed her last. When the young men came in they found her dead, and they carried her out and buried her beside her

husband. [11] And great fear came upon the whole church and upon all who heard of these things.

Many Signs and Wonders Done

[12] Now many signs and wonders were regularly done among the people by the hands of the apostles. And they were all together in Solomon's Portico. [13] None of the rest dared join them, but the people held them in high esteem. [14] And more than ever believers were added to the Lord, multitudes of both men and women, [15] so that they even carried out the sick into the streets and laid them on cots and mats, that as Peter came by at least his shadow might fall on some of them. [16] The people also gathered from the towns around Jerusalem, bringing the sick and those afflicted with unclean spirits, and they were all healed.

The Apostles Arrested and Freed

[17] But the high priest rose up, and all who were with him (that is, the party of the Sadducees), and filled with jealousy [18] they arrested the apostles and put them in the public prison. [19] But during the night an angel of the Lord opened the prison doors and brought them out, and said, [20] "Go and stand in the temple and speak to the people all the words of this Life." [21] And when they heard this, they entered the temple at daybreak and began to teach.

Now when the high priest came, and those who were with him, they called together the council, all the senate of the people of Israel, and sent to the prison to have them brought. [22] But when the officers came, they did not find them in the prison, so they returned and reported, [23] "We found the prison securely locked and the guards standing at the doors, but when

we opened them we found no one inside." **24** Now when the captain of the temple and the chief priests heard these words, they were greatly perplexed about them, wondering what this would come to. **25** And someone came and told them, "Look! The men whom you put in prison are standing in the temple and teaching the people." **26** Then the captain with the officers went and brought them, but not by force, for they were afraid of being stoned by the people.

27 And when they had brought them, they set them before the council. And the high priest questioned them, **28** saying, "We strictly charged you not to teach in this name, yet here you have filled Jerusalem with your teaching, and you intend to bring this man's blood upon us." **29** But Peter and the apostles answered, "We must obey God rather than men. **30** The God of our fathers raised Jesus, whom you killed by hanging him on a tree. **31** God exalted him at his right hand as Leader and Savior, to give repentance to Israel and forgiveness of sins. **32** And we are witnesses to these things, and so is the Holy Spirit, whom God has given to those who obey him."

33 When they heard this, they were enraged and wanted to kill them. **34** But a Pharisee in the council named Gamaliel, a teacher of the law held in honor by all the people, stood up and gave orders to put the men outside for a little while. **35** And he said to them, "Men of Israel, take care what you are about to do with these men. **36** For before these days Theudas rose up, claiming to be somebody, and a number of men, about four hundred, joined him. He was killed, and all who followed him were dispersed and came to nothing. **37** After him Judas the Galilean rose up in the days of the census and drew away some of the people after him. He too perished, and all who followed him were scattered.

³⁸ So in the present case I tell you, keep away from these men and let them alone, for if this plan or this undertaking is of man, it will fail; ³⁹ but if it is of God, you will not be able to overthrow them. You might even be found opposing God!" So they took his advice, ⁴⁰ and when they had called in the apostles, they beat them and charged them not to speak in the name of Jesus, and let them go. ⁴¹ Then they left the presence of the council, rejoicing that they were counted worthy to suffer dishonor for the name. ⁴² And every day, in the temple and from house to house, they did not cease teaching and preaching that the Christ is Jesus.

Seven Chosen to Serve

6 Now in these days when the disciples were increasing in number, a complaint by the Hellenists arose against the Hebrews because their widows were being neglected in the daily distribution. ² And the twelve summoned the full number of the disciples and said, "It is not right that we should give up preaching the word of God to serve tables. ³ Therefore, brothers, pick out from among you seven men of good repute, full of the Spirit and of wisdom, whom we will appoint to this duty. ⁴ But we will devote ourselves to prayer and to the ministry of the word." ⁵ And what they said pleased the whole gathering, and they chose Stephen, a man full of faith and of the Holy Spirit, and Philip, and Prochorus, and Nicanor, and Timon, and Parmenas, and Nicolaus, a proselyte of Antioch. ⁶ These they set before the apostles, and they prayed and laid their hands on them.

⁷ And the word of God continued to increase, and the number of the disciples multiplied greatly in Jerusalem, and a great many of the priests became obedient to the faith.

Stephen Is Seized

⁸ And Stephen, full of grace and power, was doing great wonders and signs among the people. ⁹ Then some of those who belonged to the synagogue of the Freedmen (as it was called), and of the Cyrenians, and of the Alexandrians, and of those from Cilicia and Asia, rose up and disputed with Stephen. ¹⁰ But they could not withstand the wisdom and the Spirit with which he was speaking. ¹¹ Then they secretly instigated men who said, "We have heard him speak blasphemous words against Moses and God." ¹² And they stirred up the people and the elders and the scribes, and they came upon him and seized him and brought him before the council, ¹³ and they set up false witnesses who said, "This man never ceases to speak words against this holy place and the law, ¹⁴ for we have heard him say that this Jesus of Nazareth will destroy this place and will change the customs that Moses delivered to us." ¹⁵ And gazing at him, all who sat in the council saw that his face was like the face of an angel.

Stephen's Speech

7 And the high priest said, "Are these things so?" ² And Stephen said:

"Brothers and fathers, hear me. The God of glory appeared to our father Abraham when he was in Mesopotamia, before he lived in Haran, ³ and said to him, 'Go out from your land and from your kindred and go into the land that I will show you.' ⁴ Then he went out from the land of the Chaldeans and lived in Haran. And after his father died, God removed him from there into this land in which you are now living. ⁵ Yet he gave him no inheritance in it, not even a foot's length, but promised to give

it to him as a possession and to his offspring after him, though he had no child. ⁶ And God spoke to this effect—that his offspring would be sojourners in a land belonging to others, who would enslave them and afflict them four hundred years. ⁷ 'But I will judge the nation that they serve,' said God, 'and after that they shall come out and worship me in this place.' ⁸ And he gave him the covenant of circumcision. And so Abraham became the father of Isaac, and circumcised him on the eighth day, and Isaac became the father of Jacob, and Jacob of the twelve patriarchs.

⁹ "And the patriarchs, jealous of Joseph, sold him into Egypt; but God was with him ¹⁰ and rescued him out of all his afflictions and gave him favor and wisdom before Pharaoh, king of Egypt, who made him ruler over Egypt and over all his household. ¹¹ Now there came a famine throughout all Egypt and Canaan, and great affliction, and our fathers could find no food. ¹² But when Jacob heard that there was grain in Egypt, he sent out our fathers on their first visit. ¹³ And on the second visit Joseph made himself known to his brothers, and Joseph's family became known to Pharaoh. ¹⁴ And Joseph sent and summoned Jacob his father and all his kindred, seventy-five persons in all. ¹⁵ And Jacob went down into Egypt, and he died, he and our fathers, ¹⁶ and they were carried back to Shechem and laid in the tomb that Abraham had bought for a sum of silver from the sons of Hamor in Shechem.

¹⁷ "But as the time of the promise drew near, which God had granted to Abraham, the people increased and multiplied in Egypt ¹⁸ until there arose over Egypt another king who did not know Joseph. ¹⁹ He dealt shrewdly with our race and forced our fathers to expose their infants, so that they would not be kept alive. ²⁰ At this time Moses was born; and he was beautiful in

God's sight. And he was brought up for three months in his father's house, ²¹ and when he was exposed, Pharaoh's daughter adopted him and brought him up as her own son. ²² And Moses was instructed in all the wisdom of the Egyptians, and he was mighty in his words and deeds.

²³ "When he was forty years old, it came into his heart to visit his brothers, the children of Israel. ²⁴ And seeing one of them being wronged, he defended the oppressed man and avenged him by striking down the Egyptian. ²⁵ He supposed that his brothers would understand that God was giving them salvation by his hand, but they did not understand. ²⁶ And on the following day he appeared to them as they were quarreling and tried to reconcile them, saying, 'Men, you are brothers. Why do you wrong each other?' ²⁷ But the man who was wronging his neighbor thrust him aside, saying, 'Who made you a ruler and a judge over us? ²⁸ Do you want to kill me as you killed the Egyptian yesterday?' ²⁹ At this retort Moses fled and became an exile in the land of Midian, where he became the father of two sons.

³⁰ "Now when forty years had passed, an angel appeared to him in the wilderness of Mount Sinai, in a flame of fire in a bush. ³¹ When Moses saw it, he was amazed at the sight, and as he drew near to look, there came the voice of the Lord: ³² 'I am the God of your fathers, the God of Abraham and of Isaac and of Jacob.' And Moses trembled and did not dare to look. ³³ Then the Lord said to him, 'Take off the sandals from your feet, for the place where you are standing is holy ground. ³⁴ I have surely seen the affliction of my people who are in Egypt, and have heard their groaning, and I have come down to deliver them. And now come, I will send you to Egypt.'

³⁵ "This Moses, whom they rejected, saying, 'Who made you a ruler and a judge?'—this man God sent as both ruler and redeemer by the hand of the angel who appeared to him in the bush. ³⁶ This man led them out, performing wonders and signs in Egypt and at the Red Sea and in the wilderness for forty years. ³⁷ This is the Moses who said to the Israelites, 'God will raise up for you a prophet like me from your brothers.' ³⁸ This is the one who was in the congregation in the wilderness with the angel who spoke to him at Mount Sinai, and with our fathers. He received living oracles to give to us. ³⁹ Our fathers refused to obey him, but thrust him aside, and in their hearts they turned to Egypt, ⁴⁰ saying to Aaron, 'Make for us gods who will go before us. As for this Moses who led us out from the land of Egypt, we do not know what has become of him.' ⁴¹ And they made a calf in those days, and offered a sacrifice to the idol and were rejoicing in the works of their hands. ⁴² But God turned away and gave them over to worship the host of heaven, as it is written in the book of the prophets:

> " 'Did you bring to me slain beasts and sacrifices,
>> during the forty years in the wilderness, O house
>>> of Israel?
> ⁴³   You took up the tent of Moloch
>> and the star of your god Rephan,
>> the images that you made to worship;
> and I will send you into exile beyond Babylon.'

⁴⁴ "Our fathers had the tent of witness in the wilderness, just as he who spoke to Moses directed him to make it, according to the pattern that he had seen. ⁴⁵ Our fathers in turn brought it in

with Joshua when they dispossessed the nations that God drove out before our fathers. So it was until the days of David, **46** who found favor in the sight of God and asked to find a dwelling place for the God of Jacob. **47** But it was Solomon who built a house for him. **48** Yet the Most High does not dwell in houses made by hands, as the prophet says,

49   "'Heaven is my throne,
             and the earth is my footstool.
         What kind of house will you build for me, says the
             Lord,
         or what is the place of my rest?
50   Did not my hand make all these things?'

51 "You stiff-necked people, uncircumcised in heart and ears, you always resist the Holy Spirit. As your fathers did, so do you. **52** Which of the prophets did your fathers not persecute? And they killed those who announced beforehand the coming of the Righteous One, whom you have now betrayed and murdered, **53** you who received the law as delivered by angels and did not keep it."

The Stoning of Stephen

54 Now when they heard these things they were enraged, and they ground their teeth at him. **55** But he, full of the Holy Spirit, gazed into heaven and saw the glory of God, and Jesus standing at the right hand of God. **56** And he said, "Behold, I see the heavens opened, and the Son of Man standing at the right hand of God." **57** But they cried out with a loud voice and stopped their ears and rushed together at him. **58** Then they cast him

out of the city and stoned him. And the witnesses laid down their garments at the feet of a young man named Saul. ⁵⁹ And as they were stoning Stephen, he called out, "Lord Jesus, receive my spirit." ⁶⁰ And falling to his knees he cried out with a loud voice, "Lord, do not hold this sin against them." And when he had said this, he fell asleep.

Saul Ravages the Church

8 And Saul approved of his execution.

And there arose on that day a great persecution against the church in Jerusalem, and they were all scattered throughout the regions of Judea and Samaria, except the apostles. ² Devout men buried Stephen and made great lamentation over him. ³ But Saul was ravaging the church, and entering house after house, he dragged off men and women and committed them to prison.

Philip Proclaims Christ in Samaria

⁴ Now those who were scattered went about preaching the word. ⁵ Philip went down to the city of Samaria and proclaimed to them the Christ. ⁶ And the crowds with one accord paid attention to what was being said by Philip, when they heard him and saw the signs that he did. ⁷ For unclean spirits, crying out with a loud voice, came out of many who had them, and many who were paralyzed or lame were healed. ⁸ So there was much joy in that city.

Simon the Magician Believes

⁹ But there was a man named Simon, who had previously practiced magic in the city and amazed the people of Samaria, saying that he himself was somebody great. ¹⁰ They all paid

attention to him, from the least to the greatest, saying, "This man is the power of God that is called Great." [11] And they paid attention to him because for a long time he had amazed them with his magic. [12] But when they believed Philip as he preached good news about the kingdom of God and the name of Jesus Christ, they were baptized, both men and women. [13] Even Simon himself believed, and after being baptized he continued with Philip. And seeing signs and great miracles performed, he was amazed.

[14] Now when the apostles at Jerusalem heard that Samaria had received the word of God, they sent to them Peter and John, [15] who came down and prayed for them that they might receive the Holy Spirit, [16] for he had not yet fallen on any of them, but they had only been baptized in the name of the Lord Jesus. [17] Then they laid their hands on them and they received the Holy Spirit. [18] Now when Simon saw that the Spirit was given through the laying on of the apostles' hands, he offered them money, [19] saying, "Give me this power also, so that anyone on whom I lay my hands may receive the Holy Spirit." [20] But Peter said to him, "May your silver perish with you, because you thought you could obtain the gift of God with money! [21] You have neither part nor lot in this matter, for your heart is not right before God. [22] Repent, therefore, of this wickedness of yours, and pray to the Lord that, if possible, the intent of your heart may be forgiven you. [23] For I see that you are in the gall of bitterness and in the bond of iniquity." [24] And Simon answered, "Pray for me to the Lord, that nothing of what you have said may come upon me."

[25] Now when they had testified and spoken the word of the Lord, they returned to Jerusalem, preaching the gospel to many villages of the Samaritans.

Philip and the Ethiopian Eunuch

26 Now an angel of the Lord said to Philip, "Rise and go toward the south to the road that goes down from Jerusalem to Gaza." This is a desert place. **27** And he rose and went. And there was an Ethiopian, a eunuch, a court official of Candace, queen of the Ethiopians, who was in charge of all her treasure. He had come to Jerusalem to worship **28** and was returning, seated in his chariot, and he was reading the prophet Isaiah. **29** And the Spirit said to Philip, "Go over and join this chariot." **30** So Philip ran to him and heard him reading Isaiah the prophet and asked, "Do you understand what you are reading?" **31** And he said, "How can I, unless someone guides me?" And he invited Philip to come up and sit with him. **32** Now the passage of the Scripture that he was reading was this:

> "Like a sheep he was led to the slaughter
>> and like a lamb before its shearer is silent,
>> so he opens not his mouth.
>
> **33** In his humiliation justice was denied him.
>> Who can describe his generation?
> For his life is taken away from the earth."

34 And the eunuch said to Philip, "About whom, I ask you, does the prophet say this, about himself or about someone else?" **35** Then Philip opened his mouth, and beginning with this Scripture he told him the good news about Jesus. **36** And as they were going along the road they came to some water, and the eunuch said, "See, here is water! What prevents me from being baptized?" **38** And he commanded the chariot to stop, and they both went down into the water, Philip and the eunuch, and he

baptized him. [39] And when they came up out of the water, the Spirit of the Lord carried Philip away, and the eunuch saw him no more, and went on his way rejoicing. [40] But Philip found himself at Azotus, and as he passed through he preached the gospel to all the towns until he came to Caesarea.

The Conversion of Saul

9 But Saul, still breathing threats and murder against the disciples of the Lord, went to the high priest [2] and asked him for letters to the synagogues at Damascus, so that if he found any belonging to the Way, men or women, he might bring them bound to Jerusalem. [3] Now as he went on his way, he approached Damascus, and suddenly a light from heaven shone around him. [4] And falling to the ground, he heard a voice saying to him, "Saul, Saul, why are you persecuting me?" [5] And he said, "Who are you, Lord?" And he said, "I am Jesus, whom you are persecuting. [6] But rise and enter the city, and you will be told what you are to do." [7] The men who were traveling with him stood speechless, hearing the voice but seeing no one. [8] Saul rose from the ground, and although his eyes were opened, he saw nothing. So they led him by the hand and brought him into Damascus. [9] And for three days he was without sight, and neither ate nor drank.

[10] Now there was a disciple at Damascus named Ananias. The Lord said to him in a vision, "Ananias." And he said, "Here I am, Lord." [11] And the Lord said to him, "Rise and go to the street called Straight, and at the house of Judas look for a man of Tarsus named Saul, for behold, he is praying, [12] and he has seen in a vision a man named Ananias come in and lay his hands on him so that he might regain his sight." [13] But Ananias answered,

"Lord, I have heard from many about this man, how much evil he has done to your saints at Jerusalem. [14] And here he has authority from the chief priests to bind all who call on your name." [15] But the Lord said to him, "Go, for he is a chosen instrument of mine to carry my name before the Gentiles and kings and the children of Israel. [16] For I will show him how much he must suffer for the sake of my name." [17] So Ananias departed and entered the house. And laying his hands on him he said, "Brother Saul, the Lord Jesus who appeared to you on the road by which you came has sent me so that you may regain your sight and be filled with the Holy Spirit." [18] And immediately something like scales fell from his eyes, and he regained his sight. Then he rose and was baptized; [19] and taking food, he was strengthened.

Saul Proclaims Jesus in Synagogues

For some days he was with the disciples at Damascus. [20] And immediately he proclaimed Jesus in the synagogues, saying, "He is the Son of God." [21] And all who heard him were amazed and said, "Is not this the man who made havoc in Jerusalem of those who called upon this name? And has he not come here for this purpose, to bring them bound before the chief priests?" [22] But Saul increased all the more in strength, and confounded the Jews who lived in Damascus by proving that Jesus was the Christ.

Saul Escapes from Damascus

[23] When many days had passed, the Jews plotted to kill him, [24] but their plot became known to Saul. They were watching the gates day and night in order to kill him, [25] but his disciples took him by night and let him down through an opening in the wall, lowering him in a basket.

Saul in Jerusalem

26 And when he had come to Jerusalem, he attempted to join the disciples. And they were all afraid of him, for they did not believe that he was a disciple. **27** But Barnabas took him and brought him to the apostles and declared to them how on the road he had seen the Lord, who spoke to him, and how at Damascus he had preached boldly in the name of Jesus. **28** So he went in and out among them at Jerusalem, preaching boldly in the name of the Lord. **29** And he spoke and disputed against the Hellenists. But they were seeking to kill him. **30** And when the brothers learned this, they brought him down to Caesarea and sent him off to Tarsus.

31 So the church throughout all Judea and Galilee and Samaria had peace and was being built up. And walking in the fear of the Lord and in the comfort of the Holy Spirit, it multiplied.

The Healing of Aeneas

32 Now as Peter went here and there among them all, he came down also to the saints who lived at Lydda. **33** There he found a man named Aeneas, bedridden for eight years, who was paralyzed. **34** And Peter said to him, "Aeneas, Jesus Christ heals you; rise and make your bed." And immediately he rose. **35** And all the residents of Lydda and Sharon saw him, and they turned to the Lord.

Dorcas Restored to Life

36 Now there was in Joppa a disciple named Tabitha, which, translated, means Dorcas. She was full of good works and acts of charity. **37** In those days she became ill and died, and when

they had washed her, they laid her in an upper room. **38** Since Lydda was near Joppa, the disciples, hearing that Peter was there, sent two men to him, urging him, "Please come to us without delay." **39** So Peter rose and went with them. And when he arrived, they took him to the upper room. All the widows stood beside him weeping and showing tunics and other garments that Dorcas made while she was with them. **40** But Peter put them all outside, and knelt down and prayed; and turning to the body he said, "Tabitha, arise." And she opened her eyes, and when she saw Peter she sat up. **41** And he gave her his hand and raised her up. Then, calling the saints and widows, he presented her alive. **42** And it became known throughout all Joppa, and many believed in the Lord. **43** And he stayed in Joppa for many days with one Simon, a tanner.

Peter and Cornelius

10 At Caesarea there was a man named Cornelius, a centurion of what was known as the Italian Cohort, **2** a devout man who feared God with all his household, gave alms generously to the people, and prayed continually to God. **3** About the ninth hour of the day he saw clearly in a vision an angel of God come in and say to him, "Cornelius." **4** And he stared at him in terror and said, "What is it, Lord?" And he said to him, "Your prayers and your alms have ascended as a memorial before God. **5** And now send men to Joppa and bring one Simon who is called Peter. **6** He is lodging with one Simon, a tanner, whose house is by the sea." **7** When the angel who spoke to him had departed, he called two of his servants and a devout soldier from among those who attended him, **8** and having related everything to them, he sent them to Joppa.

Peter's Vision

⁹ The next day, as they were on their journey and approaching the city, Peter went up on the housetop about the sixth hour to pray. ¹⁰ And he became hungry and wanted something to eat, but while they were preparing it, he fell into a trance ¹¹ and saw the heavens opened and something like a great sheet descending, being let down by its four corners upon the earth. ¹² In it were all kinds of animals and reptiles and birds of the air. ¹³ And there came a voice to him: "Rise, Peter; kill and eat." ¹⁴ But Peter said, "By no means, Lord; for I have never eaten anything that is common or unclean." ¹⁵ And the voice came to him again a second time, "What God has made clean, do not call common." ¹⁶ This happened three times, and the thing was taken up at once to heaven.

¹⁷ Now while Peter was inwardly perplexed as to what the vision that he had seen might mean, behold, the men who were sent by Cornelius, having made inquiry for Simon's house, stood at the gate ¹⁸ and called out to ask whether Simon who was called Peter was lodging there. ¹⁹ And while Peter was pondering the vision, the Spirit said to him, "Behold, three men are looking for you. ²⁰ Rise and go down and accompany them without hesitation, for I have sent them." ²¹ And Peter went down to the men and said, "I am the one you are looking for. What is the reason for your coming?" ²² And they said, "Cornelius, a centurion, an upright and God-fearing man, who is well spoken of by the whole Jewish nation, was directed by a holy angel to send for you to come to his house and to hear what you have to say." ²³ So he invited them in to be his guests.

The next day he rose and went away with them, and some of the brothers from Joppa accompanied him. ²⁴ And on the

following day they entered Caesarea. Cornelius was expecting them and had called together his relatives and close friends. 25 When Peter entered, Cornelius met him and fell down at his feet and worshiped him. 26 But Peter lifted him up, saying, "Stand up; I too am a man." 27 And as he talked with him, he went in and found many persons gathered. 28 And he said to them, "You yourselves know how unlawful it is for a Jew to associate with or to visit anyone of another nation, but God has shown me that I should not call any person common or unclean. 29 So when I was sent for, I came without objection. I ask then why you sent for me."

30 And Cornelius said, "Four days ago, about this hour, I was praying in my house at the ninth hour, and behold, a man stood before me in bright clothing 31 and said, 'Cornelius, your prayer has been heard and your alms have been remembered before God. 32 Send therefore to Joppa and ask for Simon who is called Peter. He is lodging in the house of Simon, a tanner, by the sea.' 33 So I sent for you at once, and you have been kind enough to come. Now therefore we are all here in the presence of God to hear all that you have been commanded by the Lord."

Gentiles Hear the Good News

34 So Peter opened his mouth and said: "Truly I understand that God shows no partiality, 35 but in every nation anyone who fears him and does what is right is acceptable to him. 36 As for the word that he sent to Israel, preaching good news of peace through Jesus Christ (he is Lord of all), 37 you yourselves know what happened throughout all Judea, beginning from Galilee after the baptism that John proclaimed: 38 how God anointed Jesus of Nazareth with the Holy Spirit and with power. He went

about doing good and healing all who were oppressed by the devil, for God was with him. ³⁹ And we are witnesses of all that he did both in the country of the Jews and in Jerusalem. They put him to death by hanging him on a tree, ⁴⁰ but God raised him on the third day and made him to appear, ⁴¹ not to all the people but to us who had been chosen by God as witnesses, who ate and drank with him after he rose from the dead. ⁴² And he commanded us to preach to the people and to testify that he is the one appointed by God to be judge of the living and the dead. ⁴³ To him all the prophets bear witness that everyone who believes in him receives forgiveness of sins through his name."

The Holy Spirit Falls on the Gentiles

⁴⁴ While Peter was still saying these things, the Holy Spirit fell on all who heard the word. ⁴⁵ And the believers from among the circumcised who had come with Peter were amazed, because the gift of the Holy Spirit was poured out even on the Gentiles. ⁴⁶ For they were hearing them speaking in tongues and extolling God. Then Peter declared, ⁴⁷ "Can anyone withhold water for baptizing these people, who have received the Holy Spirit just as we have?" ⁴⁸ And he commanded them to be baptized in the name of Jesus Christ. Then they asked him to remain for some days.

Peter Reports to the Church

11 Now the apostles and the brothers who were throughout Judea heard that the Gentiles also had received the word of God. ² So when Peter went up to Jerusalem, the circumcision party criticized him, saying, ³ "You went to uncircumcised men and ate with them." ⁴ But Peter began and explained it to them

in order: ⁵ "I was in the city of Joppa praying, and in a trance I saw a vision, something like a great sheet descending, being let down from heaven by its four corners, and it came down to me. ⁶ Looking at it closely, I observed animals and beasts of prey and reptiles and birds of the air. ⁷ And I heard a voice saying to me, 'Rise, Peter; kill and eat.' ⁸ But I said, 'By no means, Lord; for nothing common or unclean has ever entered my mouth.' ⁹ But the voice answered a second time from heaven, 'What God has made clean, do not call common.' ¹⁰ This happened three times, and all was drawn up again into heaven. ¹¹ And behold, at that very moment three men arrived at the house in which we were, sent to me from Caesarea. ¹² And the Spirit told me to go with them, making no distinction. These six brothers also accompanied me, and we entered the man's house. ¹³ And he told us how he had seen the angel stand in his house and say, 'Send to Joppa and bring Simon who is called Peter; ¹⁴ he will declare to you a message by which you will be saved, you and all your household.' ¹⁵ As I began to speak, the Holy Spirit fell on them just as on us at the beginning. ¹⁶ And I remembered the word of the Lord, how he said, 'John baptized with water, but you will be baptized with the Holy Spirit.' ¹⁷ If then God gave the same gift to them as he gave to us when we believed in the Lord Jesus Christ, who was I that I could stand in God's way?" ¹⁸ When they heard these things they fell silent. And they glorified God, saying, "Then to the Gentiles also God has granted repentance that leads to life."

The Church in Antioch

¹⁹ Now those who were scattered because of the persecution that arose over Stephen traveled as far as Phoenicia and Cyprus and Antioch, speaking the word to no one except Jews. ²⁰ But

there were some of them, men of Cyprus and Cyrene, who on coming to Antioch spoke to the Hellenists also, preaching the Lord Jesus. ²¹ And the hand of the Lord was with them, and a great number who believed turned to the Lord. ²² The report of this came to the ears of the church in Jerusalem, and they sent Barnabas to Antioch. ²³ When he came and saw the grace of God, he was glad, and he exhorted them all to remain faithful to the Lord with steadfast purpose, ²⁴ for he was a good man, full of the Holy Spirit and of faith. And a great many people were added to the Lord. ²⁵ So Barnabas went to Tarsus to look for Saul, ²⁶ and when he had found him, he brought him to Antioch. For a whole year they met with the church and taught a great many people. And in Antioch the disciples were first called Christians.

²⁷ Now in these days prophets came down from Jerusalem to Antioch. ²⁸ And one of them named Agabus stood up and foretold by the Spirit that there would be a great famine over all the world (this took place in the days of Claudius). ²⁹ So the disciples determined, every one according to his ability, to send relief to the brothers living in Judea. ³⁰ And they did so, sending it to the elders by the hand of Barnabas and Saul.

James Killed and Peter Imprisoned

12 About that time Herod the king laid violent hands on some who belonged to the church. ² He killed James the brother of John with the sword, ³ and when he saw that it pleased the Jews, he proceeded to arrest Peter also. This was during the days of Unleavened Bread. ⁴ And when he had seized him, he put him in prison, delivering him over to four squads of soldiers to guard him, intending after the Passover to bring

him out to the people. ⁵ So Peter was kept in prison, but earnest prayer for him was made to God by the church.

Peter Is Rescued

⁶ Now when Herod was about to bring him out, on that very night, Peter was sleeping between two soldiers, bound with two chains, and sentries before the door were guarding the prison. ⁷ And behold, an angel of the Lord stood next to him, and a light shone in the cell. He struck Peter on the side and woke him, saying, "Get up quickly." And the chains fell off his hands. ⁸ And the angel said to him, "Dress yourself and put on your sandals." And he did so. And he said to him, "Wrap your cloak around you and follow me." ⁹ And he went out and followed him. He did not know that what was being done by the angel was real, but thought he was seeing a vision. ¹⁰ When they had passed the first and the second guard, they came to the iron gate leading into the city. It opened for them of its own accord, and they went out and went along one street, and immediately the angel left him. ¹¹ When Peter came to himself, he said, "Now I am sure that the Lord has sent his angel and rescued me from the hand of Herod and from all that the Jewish people were expecting."

¹² When he realized this, he went to the house of Mary, the mother of John whose other name was Mark, where many were gathered together and were praying. ¹³ And when he knocked at the door of the gateway, a servant girl named Rhoda came to answer. ¹⁴ Recognizing Peter's voice, in her joy she did not open the gate but ran in and reported that Peter was standing at the gate. ¹⁵ They said to her, "You are out of your mind." But she kept insisting that it was so, and they kept saying, "It is his angel!" ¹⁶ But Peter continued knocking, and when they opened, they saw

him and were amazed. **17** But motioning to them with his hand to be silent, he described to them how the Lord had brought him out of the prison. And he said, "Tell these things to James and to the brothers." Then he departed and went to another place.

18 Now when day came, there was no little disturbance among the soldiers over what had become of Peter. **19** And after Herod searched for him and did not find him, he examined the sentries and ordered that they should be put to death. Then he went down from Judea to Caesarea and spent time there.

The Death of Herod

20 Now Herod was angry with the people of Tyre and Sidon, and they came to him with one accord, and having persuaded Blastus, the king's chamberlain, they asked for peace, because their country depended on the king's country for food. **21** On an appointed day Herod put on his royal robes, took his seat upon the throne, and delivered an oration to them. **22** And the people were shouting, "The voice of a god, and not of a man!" **23** Immediately an angel of the Lord struck him down, because he did not give God the glory, and he was eaten by worms and breathed his last.

24 But the word of God increased and multiplied.

25 And Barnabas and Saul returned from Jerusalem when they had completed their service, bringing with them John, whose other name was Mark.

Barnabas and Saul Sent Off

13 Now there were in the church at Antioch prophets and teachers, Barnabas, Simeon who was called Niger, Lucius of Cyrene, Manaen a lifelong friend of Herod the tetrarch, and

Saul. ²While they were worshiping the Lord and fasting, the Holy Spirit said, "Set apart for me Barnabas and Saul for the work to which I have called them." ³Then after fasting and praying they laid their hands on them and sent them off.

Barnabas and Saul on Cyprus

⁴So, being sent out by the Holy Spirit, they went down to Seleucia, and from there they sailed to Cyprus. ⁵When they arrived at Salamis, they proclaimed the word of God in the synagogues of the Jews. And they had John to assist them. ⁶When they had gone through the whole island as far as Paphos, they came upon a certain magician, a Jewish false prophet named Bar-Jesus. ⁷He was with the proconsul, Sergius Paulus, a man of intelligence, who summoned Barnabas and Saul and sought to hear the word of God. ⁸But Elymas the magician (for that is the meaning of his name) opposed them, seeking to turn the proconsul away from the faith. ⁹But Saul, who was also called Paul, filled with the Holy Spirit, looked intently at him ¹⁰and said, "You son of the devil, you enemy of all righteousness, full of all deceit and villainy, will you not stop making crooked the straight paths of the Lord? ¹¹And now, behold, the hand of the Lord is upon you, and you will be blind and unable to see the sun for a time." Immediately mist and darkness fell upon him, and he went about seeking people to lead him by the hand. ¹²Then the proconsul believed, when he saw what had occurred, for he was astonished at the teaching of the Lord.

Paul and Barnabas at Antioch in Pisidia

¹³Now Paul and his companions set sail from Paphos and came to Perga in Pamphylia. And John left them and returned

to Jerusalem, **14** but they went on from Perga and came to Antioch in Pisidia. And on the Sabbath day they went into the synagogue and sat down. **15** After the reading from the Law and the Prophets, the rulers of the synagogue sent a message to them, saying, "Brothers, if you have any word of encouragement for the people, say it." **16** So Paul stood up, and motioning with his hand said:

"Men of Israel and you who fear God, listen. **17** The God of this people Israel chose our fathers and made the people great during their stay in the land of Egypt, and with uplifted arm he led them out of it. **18** And for about forty years he put up with them in the wilderness. **19** And after destroying seven nations in the land of Canaan, he gave them their land as an inheritance. **20** All this took about 450 years. And after that he gave them judges until Samuel the prophet. **21** Then they asked for a king, and God gave them Saul the son of Kish, a man of the tribe of Benjamin, for forty years. **22** And when he had removed him, he raised up David to be their king, of whom he testified and said, 'I have found in David the son of Jesse a man after my heart, who will do all my will.' **23** Of this man's offspring God has brought to Israel a Savior, Jesus, as he promised. **24** Before his coming, John had proclaimed a baptism of repentance to all the people of Israel. **25** And as John was finishing his course, he said, 'What do you suppose that I am? I am not he. No, but behold, after me one is coming, the sandals of whose feet I am not worthy to untie.'

26 "Brothers, sons of the family of Abraham, and those among you who fear God, to us has been sent the message of this salvation. **27** For those who live in Jerusalem and their rulers, because they did not recognize him nor understand the

utterances of the prophets, which are read every Sabbath, fulfilled them by condemning him. ²⁸ And though they found in him no guilt worthy of death, they asked Pilate to have him executed. ²⁹ And when they had carried out all that was written of him, they took him down from the tree and laid him in a tomb. ³⁰ But God raised him from the dead, ³¹ and for many days he appeared to those who had come up with him from Galilee to Jerusalem, who are now his witnesses to the people. ³² And we bring you the good news that what God promised to the fathers, ³³ this he has fulfilled to us their children by raising Jesus, as also it is written in the second Psalm,

"'You are my Son,
    today I have begotten you.'

³⁴ And as for the fact that he raised him from the dead, no more to return to corruption, he has spoken in this way,

"'I will give you the holy and sure blessings of David.'

³⁵ Therefore he says also in another psalm,

"'You will not let your Holy One see corruption.'

³⁶ For David, after he had served the purpose of God in his own generation, fell asleep and was laid with his fathers and saw corruption, ³⁷ but he whom God raised up did not see corruption. ³⁸ Let it be known to you therefore, brothers, that through this man forgiveness of sins is proclaimed to you, ³⁹ and by him everyone who believes is freed from everything from which you

WE
Bring You
THE
GOOD
NEWS
ACTS 13:32

could not be freed by the law of Moses. [40] Beware, therefore, lest what is said in the Prophets should come about:

[41]   "'Look, you scoffers,
                be astounded and perish;
          for I am doing a work in your days,
                a work that you will not believe, even if one tells
                     it to you.'"

[42] As they went out, the people begged that these things might be told them the next Sabbath. [43] And after the meeting of the synagogue broke up, many Jews and devout converts to Judaism followed Paul and Barnabas, who, as they spoke with them, urged them to continue in the grace of God. [44] The next Sabbath almost the whole city gathered to hear the word of the Lord. [45] But when the Jews saw the crowds, they were filled with jealousy and began to contradict what was spoken by Paul, reviling him. [46] And Paul and Barnabas spoke out boldly, saying, "It was necessary that the word of God be spoken first to you. Since you thrust it aside and judge yourselves unworthy of eternal life, behold, we are turning to the Gentiles. [47] For so the Lord has commanded us, saying,

     "'I have made you a light for the Gentiles,
               that you may bring salvation to the ends of the
                    earth.'"

[48] And when the Gentiles heard this, they began rejoicing and glorifying the word of the Lord, and as many as were appointed to eternal life believed. [49] And the word of the Lord was spreading

throughout the whole region. ⁵⁰ But the Jews incited the devout women of high standing and the leading men of the city, stirred up persecution against Paul and Barnabas, and drove them out of their district. ⁵¹ But they shook off the dust from their feet against them and went to Iconium. ⁵² And the disciples were filled with joy and with the Holy Spirit.

Paul and Barnabas at Iconium

14 Now at Iconium they entered together into the Jewish synagogue and spoke in such a way that a great number of both Jews and Greeks believed. ² But the unbelieving Jews stirred up the Gentiles and poisoned their minds against the brothers. ³ So they remained for a long time, speaking boldly for the Lord, who bore witness to the word of his grace, granting signs and wonders to be done by their hands. ⁴ But the people of the city were divided; some sided with the Jews and some with the apostles. ⁵ When an attempt was made by both Gentiles and Jews, with their rulers, to mistreat them and to stone them, ⁶ they learned of it and fled to Lystra and Derbe, cities of Lycaonia, and to the surrounding country, ⁷ and there they continued to preach the gospel.

Paul and Barnabas at Lystra

⁸ Now at Lystra there was a man sitting who could not use his feet. He was crippled from birth and had never walked. ⁹ He listened to Paul speaking. And Paul, looking intently at him and seeing that he had faith to be made well, ¹⁰ said in a loud voice, "Stand upright on your feet." And he sprang up and began walking. ¹¹ And when the crowds saw what Paul had done, they lifted up their voices, saying in Lycaonian,

"The gods have come down to us in the likeness of men!" [12] Barnabas they called Zeus, and Paul, Hermes, because he was the chief speaker. [13] And the priest of Zeus, whose temple was at the entrance to the city, brought oxen and garlands to the gates and wanted to offer sacrifice with the crowds. [14] But when the apostles Barnabas and Paul heard of it, they tore their garments and rushed out into the crowd, crying out, [15] "Men, why are you doing these things? We also are men, of like nature with you, and we bring you good news, that you should turn from these vain things to a living God, who made the heaven and the earth and the sea and all that is in them. [16] In past generations he allowed all the nations to walk in their own ways. [17] Yet he did not leave himself without witness, for he did good by giving you rains from heaven and fruitful seasons, satisfying your hearts with food and gladness." [18] Even with these words they scarcely restrained the people from offering sacrifice to them.

Paul Stoned at Lystra

[19] But Jews came from Antioch and Iconium, and having persuaded the crowds, they stoned Paul and dragged him out of the city, supposing that he was dead. [20] But when the disciples gathered about him, he rose up and entered the city, and on the next day he went on with Barnabas to Derbe. [21] When they had preached the gospel to that city and had made many disciples, they returned to Lystra and to Iconium and to Antioch, [22] strengthening the souls of the disciples, encouraging them to continue in the faith, and saying that through many tribulations we must enter the kingdom of God. [23] And when they had appointed elders for them in every church, with prayer and

fasting they committed them to the Lord in whom they had believed.

Paul and Barnabas Return to Antioch in Syria

²⁴ Then they passed through Pisidia and came to Pamphylia. ²⁵ And when they had spoken the word in Perga, they went down to Attalia, ²⁶ and from there they sailed to Antioch, where they had been commended to the grace of God for the work that they had fulfilled. ²⁷ And when they arrived and gathered the church together, they declared all that God had done with them, and how he had opened a door of faith to the Gentiles. ²⁸ And they remained no little time with the disciples.

The Jerusalem Council

15 But some men came down from Judea and were teaching the brothers, "Unless you are circumcised according to the custom of Moses, you cannot be saved." ² And after Paul and Barnabas had no small dissension and debate with them, Paul and Barnabas and some of the others were appointed to go up to Jerusalem to the apostles and the elders about this question. ³ So, being sent on their way by the church, they passed through both Phoenicia and Samaria, describing in detail the conversion of the Gentiles, and brought great joy to all the brothers. ⁴ When they came to Jerusalem, they were welcomed by the church and the apostles and the elders, and they declared all that God had done with them. ⁵ But some believers who belonged to the party of the Pharisees rose up and said, "It is necessary to circumcise them and to order them to keep the law of Moses."

⁶ The apostles and the elders were gathered together to consider this matter. ⁷ And after there had been much debate, Peter

stood up and said to them, "Brothers, you know that in the early days God made a choice among you, that by my mouth the Gentiles should hear the word of the gospel and believe. ⁸ And God, who knows the heart, bore witness to them, by giving them the Holy Spirit just as he did to us, ⁹ and he made no distinction between us and them, having cleansed their hearts by faith. ¹⁰ Now, therefore, why are you putting God to the test by placing a yoke on the neck of the disciples that neither our fathers nor we have been able to bear? ¹¹ But we believe that we will be saved through the grace of the Lord Jesus, just as they will."

¹² And all the assembly fell silent, and they listened to Barnabas and Paul as they related what signs and wonders God had done through them among the Gentiles. ¹³ After they finished speaking, James replied, "Brothers, listen to me. ¹⁴ Simeon has related how God first visited the Gentiles, to take from them a people for his name. ¹⁵ And with this the words of the prophets agree, just as it is written,

¹⁶   "'After this I will return,
        and I will rebuild the tent of David that has fallen;
        I will rebuild its ruins,
            and I will restore it,
¹⁷   that the remnant of mankind may seek the Lord,
            and all the Gentiles who are called by my name,
        says the Lord, who makes these things ¹⁸ known
            from of old.'

¹⁹ Therefore my judgment is that we should not trouble those of the Gentiles who turn to God, ²⁰ but should write to them

to abstain from the things polluted by idols, and from sexual immorality, and from what has been strangled, and from blood. ²¹ For from ancient generations Moses has had in every city those who proclaim him, for he is read every Sabbath in the synagogues."

The Council's Letter to Gentile Believers

²² Then it seemed good to the apostles and the elders, with the whole church, to choose men from among them and send them to Antioch with Paul and Barnabas. They sent Judas called Barsabbas, and Silas, leading men among the brothers, ²³ with the following letter: "The brothers, both the apostles and the elders, to the brothers who are of the Gentiles in Antioch and Syria and Cilicia, greetings. ²⁴ Since we have heard that some persons have gone out from us and troubled you with words, unsettling your minds, although we gave them no instructions, ²⁵ it has seemed good to us, having come to one accord, to choose men and send them to you with our beloved Barnabas and Paul, ²⁶ men who have risked their lives for the name of our Lord Jesus Christ. ²⁷ We have therefore sent Judas and Silas, who themselves will tell you the same things by word of mouth. ²⁸ For it has seemed good to the Holy Spirit and to us to lay on you no greater burden than these requirements: ²⁹ that you abstain from what has been sacrificed to idols, and from blood, and from what has been strangled, and from sexual immorality. If you keep yourselves from these, you will do well. Farewell."

³⁰ So when they were sent off, they went down to Antioch, and having gathered the congregation together, they delivered the letter. ³¹ And when they had read it, they rejoiced because

of its encouragement. ³² And Judas and Silas, who were themselves prophets, encouraged and strengthened the brothers with many words. ³³ And after they had spent some time, they were sent off in peace by the brothers to those who had sent them. ³⁵ But Paul and Barnabas remained in Antioch, teaching and preaching the word of the Lord, with many others also.

Paul and Barnabas Separate

³⁶ And after some days Paul said to Barnabas, "Let us return and visit the brothers in every city where we proclaimed the word of the Lord, and see how they are." ³⁷ Now Barnabas wanted to take with them John called Mark. ³⁸ But Paul thought best not to take with them one who had withdrawn from them in Pamphylia and had not gone with them to the work. ³⁹ And there arose a sharp disagreement, so that they separated from each other. Barnabas took Mark with him and sailed away to Cyprus, ⁴⁰ but Paul chose Silas and departed, having been commended by the brothers to the grace of the Lord. ⁴¹ And he went through Syria and Cilicia, strengthening the churches.

Timothy Joins Paul and Silas

16 Paul came also to Derbe and to Lystra. A disciple was there, named Timothy, the son of a Jewish woman who was a believer, but his father was a Greek. ² He was well spoken of by the brothers at Lystra and Iconium. ³ Paul wanted Timothy to accompany him, and he took him and circumcised him because of the Jews who were in those places, for they all knew that his father was a Greek. ⁴ As they went on their way through the cities, they delivered to them for observance the

decisions that had been reached by the apostles and elders who were in Jerusalem. ⁵ So the churches were strengthened in the faith, and they increased in numbers daily.

The Macedonian Call

⁶ And they went through the region of Phrygia and Galatia, having been forbidden by the Holy Spirit to speak the word in Asia. ⁷ And when they had come up to Mysia, they attempted to go into Bithynia, but the Spirit of Jesus did not allow them. ⁸ So, passing by Mysia, they went down to Troas. ⁹ And a vision appeared to Paul in the night: a man of Macedonia was standing there, urging him and saying, "Come over to Macedonia and help us." ¹⁰ And when Paul had seen the vision, immediately we sought to go on into Macedonia, concluding that God had called us to preach the gospel to them.

The Conversion of Lydia

¹¹ So, setting sail from Troas, we made a direct voyage to Samothrace, and the following day to Neapolis, ¹² and from there to Philippi, which is a leading city of the district of Macedonia and a Roman colony. We remained in this city some days. ¹³ And on the Sabbath day we went outside the gate to the riverside, where we supposed there was a place of prayer, and we sat down and spoke to the women who had come together. ¹⁴ One who heard us was a woman named Lydia, from the city of Thyatira, a seller of purple goods, who was a worshiper of God. The Lord opened her heart to pay attention to what was said by Paul. ¹⁵ And after she was baptized, and her household as well, she urged us, saying, "If you have judged me to be faithful to the Lord, come to my house and stay." And she prevailed upon us.

Paul and Silas in Prison

16 As we were going to the place of prayer, we were met by a slave girl who had a spirit of divination and brought her owners much gain by fortune-telling. **17** She followed Paul and us, crying out, "These men are servants of the Most High God, who proclaim to you the way of salvation." **18** And this she kept doing for many days. Paul, having become greatly annoyed, turned and said to the spirit, "I command you in the name of Jesus Christ to come out of her." And it came out that very hour.

19 But when her owners saw that their hope of gain was gone, they seized Paul and Silas and dragged them into the marketplace before the rulers. **20** And when they had brought them to the magistrates, they said, "These men are Jews, and they are disturbing our city. **21** They advocate customs that are not lawful for us as Romans to accept or practice." **22** The crowd joined in attacking them, and the magistrates tore the garments off them and gave orders to beat them with rods. **23** And when they had inflicted many blows upon them, they threw them into prison, ordering the jailer to keep them safely. **24** Having received this order, he put them into the inner prison and fastened their feet in the stocks.

The Philippian Jailer Converted

25 About midnight Paul and Silas were praying and singing hymns to God, and the prisoners were listening to them, **26** and suddenly there was a great earthquake, so that the foundations of the prison were shaken. And immediately all the doors were opened, and everyone's bonds were unfastened. **27** When the jailer woke and saw that the prison doors were open, he drew his sword and was about to kill himself, supposing that the

against him. ¹⁶ I answered them that it was not the custom of the Romans to give up anyone before the accused met the accusers face to face and had opportunity to make his defense concerning the charge laid against him. ¹⁷ So when they came together here, I made no delay, but on the next day took my seat on the tribunal and ordered the man to be brought. ¹⁸ When the accusers stood up, they brought no charge in his case of such evils as I supposed. ¹⁹ Rather they had certain points of dispute with him about their own religion and about a certain Jesus, who was dead, but whom Paul asserted to be alive. ²⁰ Being at a loss how to investigate these questions, I asked whether he wanted to go to Jerusalem and be tried there regarding them. ²¹ But when Paul had appealed to be kept in custody for the decision of the emperor, I ordered him to be held until I could send him to Caesar." ²² Then Agrippa said to Festus, "I would like to hear the man myself." "Tomorrow," said he, "you will hear him."

²³ So on the next day Agrippa and Bernice came with great pomp, and they entered the audience hall with the military tribunes and the prominent men of the city. Then, at the command of Festus, Paul was brought in. ²⁴ And Festus said, "King Agrippa and all who are present with us, you see this man about whom the whole Jewish people petitioned me, both in Jerusalem and here, shouting that he ought not to live any longer. ²⁵ But I found that he had done nothing deserving death. And as he himself appealed to the emperor, I decided to go ahead and send him. ²⁶ But I have nothing definite to write to my lord about him. Therefore I have brought him before you all, and especially before you, King Agrippa, so that, after we have examined him, I may have something to write. ²⁷ For it

Paul Tells of His Conversion

[12] "In this connection I journeyed to Damascus with the authority and commission of the chief priests. [13] At midday, O king, I saw on the way a light from heaven, brighter than the sun, that shone around me and those who journeyed with me. [14] And when we had all fallen to the ground, I heard a voice saying to me in the Hebrew language, 'Saul, Saul, why are you persecuting me? It is hard for you to kick against the goads.' [15] And I said, 'Who are you, Lord?' And the Lord said, 'I am Jesus whom you are persecuting. [16] But rise and stand upon your feet, for I have appeared to you for this purpose, to appoint you as a servant and witness to the things in which you have seen me and to those in which I will appear to you, [17] delivering you from your people and from the Gentiles—to whom I am sending you [18] to open their eyes, so that they may turn from darkness to light and from the power of Satan to God, that they may receive forgiveness of sins and a place among those who are sanctified by faith in me.'

[19] "Therefore, O King Agrippa, I was not disobedient to the heavenly vision, [20] but declared first to those in Damascus, then in Jerusalem and throughout all the region of Judea, and also to the Gentiles, that they should repent and turn to God, performing deeds in keeping with their repentance. [21] For this reason the Jews seized me in the temple and tried to kill me. [22] To this day I have had the help that comes from God, and so I stand here testifying both to small and great, saying nothing but what the prophets and Moses said would come to pass: [23] that the Christ must suffer and that, by being the first to rise from the dead, he would proclaim light both to our people and to the Gentiles."

²⁴ And as he was saying these things in his defense, Festus said with a loud voice, "Paul, you are out of your mind; your great learning is driving you out of your mind." ²⁵ But Paul said, "I am not out of my mind, most excellent Festus, but I am speaking true and rational words. ²⁶ For the king knows about these things, and to him I speak boldly. For I am persuaded that none of these things has escaped his notice, for this has not been done in a corner. ²⁷ King Agrippa, do you believe the prophets? I know that you believe." ²⁸ And Agrippa said to Paul, "In a short time would you persuade me to be a Christian?" ²⁹ And Paul said, "Whether short or long, I would to God that not only you but also all who hear me this day might become such as I am—except for these chains."

³⁰ Then the king rose, and the governor and Bernice and those who were sitting with them. ³¹ And when they had withdrawn, they said to one another, "This man is doing nothing to deserve death or imprisonment." ³² And Agrippa said to Festus, "This man could have been set free if he had not appealed to Caesar."

Paul Sails for Rome

27 And when it was decided that we should sail for Italy, they delivered Paul and some other prisoners to a centurion of the Augustan Cohort named Julius. ² And embarking in a ship of Adramyttium, which was about to sail to the ports along the coast of Asia, we put to sea, accompanied by Aristarchus, a Macedonian from Thessalonica. ³ The next day we put in at Sidon. And Julius treated Paul kindly and gave him leave to go to his friends and be cared for. ⁴ And putting out to sea from there we sailed under the lee of Cyprus, because the

winds were against us. ⁵ And when we had sailed across the open sea along the coast of Cilicia and Pamphylia, we came to Myra in Lycia. ⁶ There the centurion found a ship of Alexandria sailing for Italy and put us on board. ⁷ We sailed slowly for a number of days and arrived with difficulty off Cnidus, and as the wind did not allow us to go farther, we sailed under the lee of Crete off Salmone. ⁸ Coasting along it with difficulty, we came to a place called Fair Havens, near which was the city of Lasea.

⁹ Since much time had passed, and the voyage was now dangerous because even the Fast was already over, Paul advised them, ¹⁰ saying, "Sirs, I perceive that the voyage will be with injury and much loss, not only of the cargo and the ship, but also of our lives." ¹¹ But the centurion paid more attention to the pilot and to the owner of the ship than to what Paul said. ¹² And because the harbor was not suitable to spend the winter in, the majority decided to put out to sea from there, on the chance that somehow they could reach Phoenix, a harbor of Crete, facing both southwest and northwest, and spend the winter there.

The Storm at Sea

¹³ Now when the south wind blew gently, supposing that they had obtained their purpose, they weighed anchor and sailed along Crete, close to the shore. ¹⁴ But soon a tempestuous wind, called the northeaster, struck down from the land. ¹⁵ And when the ship was caught and could not face the wind, we gave way to it and were driven along. ¹⁶ Running under the lee of a small island called Cauda, we managed with difficulty to secure the ship's boat. ¹⁷ After hoisting it up, they used supports to undergird the ship. Then, fearing that they would run aground on the Syrtis, they lowered the gear, and thus they were driven

along. ¹⁸ Since we were violently storm-tossed, they began the next day to jettison the cargo. ¹⁹ And on the third day they threw the ship's tackle overboard with their own hands. ²⁰ When neither sun nor stars appeared for many days, and no small tempest lay on us, all hope of our being saved was at last abandoned.

²¹ Since they had been without food for a long time, Paul stood up among them and said, "Men, you should have listened to me and not have set sail from Crete and incurred this injury and loss. ²² Yet now I urge you to take heart, for there will be no loss of life among you, but only of the ship. ²³ For this very night there stood before me an angel of the God to whom I belong and whom I worship, ²⁴ and he said, 'Do not be afraid, Paul; you must stand before Caesar. And behold, God has granted you all those who sail with you.' ²⁵ So take heart, men, for I have faith in God that it will be exactly as I have been told. ²⁶ But we must run aground on some island."

²⁷ When the fourteenth night had come, as we were being driven across the Adriatic Sea, about midnight the sailors suspected that they were nearing land. ²⁸ So they took a sounding and found twenty fathoms. A little farther on they took a sounding again and found fifteen fathoms. ²⁹ And fearing that we might run on the rocks, they let down four anchors from the stern and prayed for day to come. ³⁰ And as the sailors were seeking to escape from the ship, and had lowered the ship's boat into the sea under pretense of laying out anchors from the bow, ³¹ Paul said to the centurion and the soldiers, "Unless these men stay in the ship, you cannot be saved." ³² Then the soldiers cut away the ropes of the ship's boat and let it go.

³³ As day was about to dawn, Paul urged them all to take some food, saying, "Today is the fourteenth day that you have

continued in suspense and without food, having taken nothing. ³⁴ Therefore I urge you to take some food. For it will give you strength, for not a hair is to perish from the head of any of you." ³⁵ And when he had said these things, he took bread, and giving thanks to God in the presence of all he broke it and began to eat. ³⁶ Then they all were encouraged and ate some food themselves. ³⁷ (We were in all 276 persons in the ship.) ³⁸ And when they had eaten enough, they lightened the ship, throwing out the wheat into the sea.

The Shipwreck

³⁹ Now when it was day, they did not recognize the land, but they noticed a bay with a beach, on which they planned if possible to run the ship ashore. ⁴⁰ So they cast off the anchors and left them in the sea, at the same time loosening the ropes that tied the rudders. Then hoisting the foresail to the wind they made for the beach. ⁴¹ But striking a reef, they ran the vessel aground. The bow stuck and remained immovable, and the stern was being broken up by the surf. ⁴² The soldiers' plan was to kill the prisoners, lest any should swim away and escape. ⁴³ But the centurion, wishing to save Paul, kept them from carrying out their plan. He ordered those who could swim to jump overboard first and make for the land, ⁴⁴ and the rest on planks or on pieces of the ship. And so it was that all were brought safely to land.

Paul on Malta

28 After we were brought safely through, we then learned that the island was called Malta. ² The native people showed us unusual kindness, for they kindled a fire and welcomed us all, because it had begun to rain and was cold.

³ When Paul had gathered a bundle of sticks and put them on the fire, a viper came out because of the heat and fastened on his hand. ⁴ When the native people saw the creature hanging from his hand, they said to one another, "No doubt this man is a murderer. Though he has escaped from the sea, Justice has not allowed him to live." ⁵ He, however, shook off the creature into the fire and suffered no harm. ⁶ They were waiting for him to swell up or suddenly fall down dead. But when they had waited a long time and saw no misfortune come to him, they changed their minds and said that he was a god.

⁷ Now in the neighborhood of that place were lands belonging to the chief man of the island, named Publius, who received us and entertained us hospitably for three days. ⁸ It happened that the father of Publius lay sick with fever and dysentery. And Paul visited him and prayed, and putting his hands on him, healed him. ⁹ And when this had taken place, the rest of the people on the island who had diseases also came and were cured. ¹⁰ They also honored us greatly, and when we were about to sail, they put on board whatever we needed.

Paul Arrives at Rome

¹¹ After three months we set sail in a ship that had wintered in the island, a ship of Alexandria, with the twin gods as a figurehead. ¹² Putting in at Syracuse, we stayed there for three days. ¹³ And from there we made a circuit and arrived at Rhegium. And after one day a south wind sprang up, and on the second day we came to Puteoli. ¹⁴ There we found brothers and were invited to stay with them for seven days. And so we came to Rome. ¹⁵ And the brothers there, when they heard about us, came as far as the Forum of Appius and Three Taverns

to meet us. On seeing them, Paul thanked God and took courage. ¹⁶ And when we came into Rome, Paul was allowed to stay by himself, with the soldier who guarded him.

Paul in Rome

¹⁷ After three days he called together the local leaders of the Jews, and when they had gathered, he said to them, "Brothers, though I had done nothing against our people or the customs of our fathers, yet I was delivered as a prisoner from Jerusalem into the hands of the Romans. ¹⁸ When they had examined me, they wished to set me at liberty, because there was no reason for the death penalty in my case. ¹⁹ But because the Jews objected, I was compelled to appeal to Caesar—though I had no charge to bring against my nation. ²⁰ For this reason, therefore, I have asked to see you and speak with you, since it is because of the hope of Israel that I am wearing this chain." ²¹ And they said to him, "We have received no letters from Judea about you, and none of the brothers coming here has reported or spoken any evil about you. ²² But we desire to hear from you what your views are, for with regard to this sect we know that everywhere it is spoken against."

²³ When they had appointed a day for him, they came to him at his lodging in greater numbers. From morning till evening he expounded to them, testifying to the kingdom of God and trying to convince them about Jesus both from the Law of Moses and from the Prophets. ²⁴ And some were convinced by what he said, but others disbelieved. ²⁵ And disagreeing among themselves, they departed after Paul had made one statement: "The Holy Spirit was right in saying to your fathers through Isaiah the prophet:

26   "'Go to this people, and say,
> "You will indeed hear but never understand,
>> and you will indeed see but never perceive."

27   For this people's heart has grown dull,
>> and with their ears they can barely hear,
>> and their eyes they have closed;
> lest they should see with their eyes
>> and hear with their ears
> and understand with their heart
>> and turn, and I would heal them.'

28 Therefore let it be known to you that this salvation of God has been sent to the Gentiles; they will listen."

30 He lived there two whole years at his own expense, and welcomed all who came to him, 31 proclaiming the kingdom of God and teaching about the Lord Jesus Christ with all boldness and without hindrance.